7 Myths About Money

What You Think You Know About Money Will Bankrupt You

By Todd Coontz

7 Myths About Money: What You Think You Know About Money Will Bankrupt You

ISBN 1-891-734-31-8

ROCKWEALTH MINISTRIES
P.O. Box 6177
Aiken, South Carolina 29804-6177

Printed in the United States of America.

Editorial Content and Design – Deborah Murdock Johnson
Book Cover Design – Bryant Design
Printed By – Faith Printing, Inc.

~ *Special Notice* ~

The information in this book is given in accordance with the following statement:

The purpose and intent of this book is to help the readers to identify the way they think about money. This book is not intended to give any specific advice on the subjects of investment, insurance, legal or accounting practices. It is intended to provide advice on ways and means of overcoming a mentality that disrespects money.

These suggestions are based on a religious belief system and scriptural concepts are used to illustrate each point. No two financial situations are exactly alike. **Always seek professional counsel before making changes in your financial matters.**

The information contained in this book is, to the author's knowledge, conceptually correct. The author and publisher and their representatives shall not be held liable for actions taken by those who do not seek professional advice.

~ *Foreword* ~

Money matters.

Money builds churches, schools, colleges, hospitals. It clothes orphans and feeds the hungry. It is a weapon against the adversary of inferiority. It is a tool that sculptures every desired environment. It is a Bridge from Disasters to Dreams. It is a Vehicle for Victorious Accomplishments.

That's why I'm *glad* Todd Coontz wrote this book.

It will *rekindle* the flickering flame in those who are burned out. It will *correct* the misconceptions many have about financial freedom. It will *motivate* those who have felt guilty or embarrassed at having great goals and dreams.

Todd is more than a very successful millionaire businessman. He is obsessed with helping those living in financial torment to step into total financial victory. He *loves* people. He *hates* pain. His pure heart and deep passion for *Wisdom* will link him to thousands who need this Word of Victory.

It is a *privilege* to commend this "Young Champion of the Faith" to the Body of Christ. May the Holy Spirit use this book as His Instrument of *Wisdom* to Unlock Your Next Season of Prosperity.

Pursuing Wisdom,
Dr. Mike Murdock

~ *Acknowledgments* ~

I have been fortunate to have had three mentors during my lifetime. Because of them, the shaping of my character and development of my walk with Christ has flourished.

Bud Marshall — Who introduced me to Christ and also spent countless hours *teaching* me His principles;

Cesar Brooks — My pastor of ten years, who has become both a *good friend* and a practical source of wisdom from which to draw;

Dr. Mike Murdock — Who is a *master polisher* and a loyal friend whose *wisdom* challenges me to be more than what I am.

To all of you, thank you for your love, your wisdom and your encouragement.

~ *Special Thanks* ~

First Family Church of Augusta — Pastor Cesar & Sherry Brooks

Agape Worship Center — Pastor Jesse & Dedee Tipton

Abundant Life Church — Pastor Wilson Soko

Lamb Broadcasting, Inc. — Charles Reed, Founder

Watchmen Broadcasting, Inc. — Russell & Dorothy Spaulding

ACME Restoration — Owner Paul & April Babb

Automotive Excellence — Owner John & Cecil Albert

Pine Log Machine & Welding, Inc. — Owner Alvin Tipton

Jesse & Dedee Tipton
Homer & Teresa Gilbreath
Cubie M. Oglesbee
Herb & Sherrell Sizemore
Mark & Jeanie Sczublewski
Donnella Wesley
Judith Dunning
Pastor Ralph Cruze
Landon Coontz
Lara K. Walker
David & Tammy Wapshop
Clarence C. Wright
Brenda M. Threatt
Natalie D. Ferguson
John & Neva Hollins
Diana King
Anilda Leiva

~ Dedication ~

This book would not be possible if it were not for my parents, *William J. Coontz* and *Sara M. Coontz.*

My father's love, acceptance and willingness to give of his *time* provided the foundation on which I built my understanding of what it means to be a man. I learned the importance of strength...a *strength* that stands in the most severe storms. I only witnessed my father's tears three times in my lifetime, each making a significant impact on my life. The night he surrendered to Jesus, the day he left me at Bible College, and the day I left home to live on my own. These times taught me the strength of a man is found not in his ability to cover his tears, but in his resolve to share his emotions while standing firm.

My mother's *unfailing belief* in her son and constant encouragement has brought me to where I am today. I can still hear my mother saying to me daily as I was growing up, "Todd, you can be anything, you can do anything, and nothing is impossible for you with God on your side." She recognized in me potential that was hidden to the eyes of others. My success has come because I sat at the feet of a mother who was loving, patient and the most giving person I have ever met. My mother is truly a *Proverbs 31 Woman.*

My wife, who taught me what it means to give with no strings attached. Her love is unfailing and her heart is tender... she is my *best friend.*

My son, Landon, who is the *apple* of my eye and who teaches me each day about God's love for His children.

~ *Introduction* ~

The reason I wrote this book is to *motivate* you to change the way you think about money. Your belief system always determines your actions. Your actions will determine your wealth! **What you *think* about money matters.** You can only attract what you respect. The wealthy have more money because they respect money.

Are you tired of being broke? Are the bills and credit card debts stacking up? Do you feel like giving up financially? There is hope! The information contained in this book will change your **financial destiny!** What you believe is based on the information you've learned. *Right results will never be birthed from the wrong information.* To get different results, you must *replace* wrong information with corrected information. When you do this, you will *develop* a **healthy mentality** that respects money, therefore giving money permission to come into your life.

Over twelve years ago, I had nothing. My mind-set disrespected money. Although I knew the truth, I really had never practiced the scriptural principles about *giving* and financial prosperity. I *hate* poverty. I *love* people. My life changed the day I started giving a portion of my money to God. The principle of **seed...time...harvest** has taken me from nothing to financial freedom. On my journey, I have made mistakes, yet by observation and through diligent studies about the rich, I have learned some of their principles and secrets for attracting money. I believe all wealth has been the result of **Biblical principles.** I want to share these *principles* I have learned with you, so you too can find the freedom I now enjoy.

~ ***Todd Coontz***

~ *Table of Contents* ~

The Size of Your
Bank Account
Does Not Determine
Your Love for Money.

~~~

I Have Met As Many
Poor People
Who Love Money
As Rich People.

~ *Todd Coontz* ~

~~~

Myth #1

Money Is the Root Of All Evil

In this book, you will learn that much of what you have believed about money has been a lie, or worse…a half-truth! Your actions are always the direct result of your belief system. What you believe is based on the information you have learned. ***Right results will never be birthed from the wrong information!*** If you are expecting different results you must replace wrong information with corrected information. The myth "money is the root of all evil" is founded on a misquoted verse in the Bible that correctly reads:

> ***For the love of money*** *is the root of all evil: which while some coveted after, they have erred from the faith, and pierced themselves with many sorrows.*
>
> *1 Timothy 6:10*

The *love* of money, not money itself, is the root of all evil. In fact, the word *love* in this message is more accurately defined as lust. Read 1 Corinthians, chapter 13, verse 8: "Love never faileth…." If love never fails then how could the love of money be the root of all sin? It can't. Lust is the root of all sin. Lust originated from the very beginning through the birth of a lie that Lucifer deceived himself in thinking he could become God.

If lust was the original sin then it would be reasonable to assume that money is not the root of all evil. Lucifer sinned because he lusted after God's throne. Adam and Eve sinned because they were deceived by the serpent who promised them that they would be equal to God. Neither Lucifer nor Adam fell because of their love of money. Sodom and Gomorrah were sentenced to destruction by fire and this wasn't over money. King David committed murder and Samson and Delilah committed fornication. Neither could blame money for their sins. They all sinned because of the original sin…lust. None of them sinned because of the **love of money.**

All people do not love money. Some lust after money, allowing it to control their lives. The size of your bank account does not determine whether you will love money or not. *I have met as many poor people who loved money as rich people*. Rich people love it because they have it and the poor love it because they wish they had it. Anything that you love more than God becomes an idol, and therefore is wrong. When the Apostle Paul was writing to Timothy, he was not condemning money, but rather admonishing him not to covet or lust after it.

For years, Christians have believed that having money was evil and that too much of it would cause them to backslide, therefore missing out on heaven. Many Christians who love God and dedicate their time and efforts to promote God's work **unknowingly** sabotage their financial blessings. They do this because they believe it is wrong to have money. They will often find themselves in financial lack because of their belief system and then wonder why God does not bless them with money.

Ask yourself this question: *"If money was so evil and having it would be all that it would take for me to turn my back on God, then why doesn't the devil give me more money?"* Because financial worry is devastating to your life! When you are worried about how you are going to pay your bills it distracts you and causes you to lose your focus on God's goodness. When the devil convinces you that God wants you to be broke, and God doesn't really care about you, he robs God of His greatest pleasure...to give. God is willing to give to you, and has made available His riches. Consider this: When the devil attacked the life of Job, he took all of his wealth away from him. The devil left him devastated financially! It was God who gave back and restored Job's wealth...*twofold!*

What you believe about money will determine how you react towards it. ***Your financial increase is determined by the level of respect you have for money.*** Your respect for money will dictate your actions. If you believe that money is the root of all evil then you will act in such a way to keep yourself from getting any of it. In your *subconscious* mind, you will think money will harm you and keep you from serving God. Your actions toward money will be negative and money will move away from you instead of moving towards you.

"You Can Only Attract What You Respect."
Dr. Mike Murdock

Anything that you do not respect will eventually move away from your life! If you respect doctors you will seek their help when you are sick. If you respect mechanics you will call them to repair your car when it breaks down. If you respect your boss you will go out of your way to help him. If you respect money, then you will seek financial counsel from those who are qualified to help you, such as your CPA or financial advisor.

If I can help exchange wrong information with right information, therefore replacing a myth for the truth, your thoughts about money will change too. You will then develop a mentality of respect towards money and therefore do the things necessary to attract money into your life. *What is conceived in your mind will come to pass in time.*

You are what you think about. You cannot move beyond your thought process. You will naturally move in the direction of your most dominant thought concerning what you believe and which picture has been painted in your mind. For example, if you tell your child not to play in the road where is he probably going to go? More than likely he will go play in the road. Why? Because the *picture* that is most dominant in his mind is the road. But, instead of instructing him not to play in the road, you say to him, "Go and play in the backyard." Where is he going now? The backyard. If you want to change where he is going, you have to paint a different picture in his mind. When he imagines the back yard with green grass, sand boxes, and a swing set this picture will cause him to gravitate toward your instructions. *How you view money and what you think about money is no exception, and your thoughts will move you toward it or away from it.*

> *For as a man thinketh in his heart, so is he....*
> *Proverbs 23:7*

From the very beginning of time God's will has been to prosper and take care of His children. When He created Adam and Eve, He placed them in a garden filled with abundance. Remember, the Garden in Eden was created for Adam and Eve; they were not created for the garden. The reason for this was that God was displaying His love to *give* before He created man. God's very nature is to give to His children!

> *And God blessed them, and God said unto them, be fruitful and multiply, and replenish the earth, and subdue it: and have dominion over the fish of the sea, and over the fowl of the air, and over every living thing that moveth upon the earth.*

And God said, Behold, I have given you every herb bearing seed, which is upon the face of the earth, and every tree in which is the fruit of the tree yielding seed: to you it shall be for meat.

Genesis 1:28-29

God provided abundance for Adam and Eve and they did not have any wants that God did not provide. What a Paradise! It must have been something spectacular - in the evening time God Himself would walk with them in the Garden enjoying their fellowship. It is so tragic that so many believe God wants them to be poor, and that living a life of poverty brings pleasure to Him. When we believe this teaching we are robbing God of His greatest pleasure which is **giving** to His children.

The young lions do lack, and suffer hunger: but they that seek the Lord shall not want any good thing.

Psalms 34:10

He that spared not his own Son, but delivered him up for us all, how shall he not with Him also freely give us all things?

Romans 8:32

If you then, being evil, know how to give good gifts unto your children, how much more shall your Father which is in heaven give good things to them that ask Him?

Matthew 7:11

We must understand that God created everything in heaven and on the earth. However, God's finest masterpiece was mankind. Man was not just another creative work of God, but sculptured in His likeness. Man was given *free volition* and was capable of making his own decisions.

And God created man in his own image, in the image of God created he him; male and female created he them.
Genesis 1:27

God placed Adam and Eve in the Garden for them to enjoy what He had provided. He provided abundance through a variety of trees, fruits, and vegetation. God granted permission to man allowing him to eat of all of them but one. In fact, God commanded them to eat not of the tree of knowledge of good and evil. The Bible says that the serpent came into the garden and tempted Adam and Eve to eat of the forbidden tree.

And the woman said unto the serpent, we may eat of the fruit of the trees of the garden: but the fruit of the tree in the midst of the garden, God hath said, Ye shall not eat of it, neither shall ye touch it lest ye shall die.
Genesis 3:3

Half-truths are deadly. Eve misquoted God. God never instructed her not to touch the tree. He only commanded them not to eat from the tree. It is important to recognize that in order for truth to exist it must be accurate. Half-truth consists of truth that is inaccurate leaving out important details. *Half-truth is inaccurate truth!* Most people find themselves impoverished, not because they are doing everything wrong, but because of the one thing they're not doing right. You can buy a brand new Lexus LS 430, but when you remove one tire you're not going anywhere!

Adam and Eve were disobedient when they ate of the forbidden tree. Their eyes were opened and sin entered into the human race from the original sin…lust. God created everything. There is nothing that is not in His sovereign control. I have been asked many times, "Why did God place the tree of good and evil in the garden?" I have often asked myself that question,

"Wouldn't life be much simpler if He only left that tree out?" True, except that God wanted a relationship with mankind. The only way to have this was to give man the freedom of choice. God wanted man to choose Him. The only way that this could be accomplished was to give mankind the ability to choose. This is why to love or choose something over God displeases Him.

The only thing we have to truly offer God is our ***obedience.*** He is searching for people to be obedient to His instructions. He even told King Saul that *obedience* was better than sacrifice. Think about this for a moment: What sacrifice can you offer God that would be worthy for Him to receive? What do you possess that He doesn't have or can not create? Nothing! But, He has chosen to give you free will to choose and the freedom to make decisions based on what you believe. Will you choose to be obedient? God wants you to use your money to do good things and He desires for your needs to be supplied. This gives Him pleasure to be believed and when we acknowledge His goodness by our *obedience* He is pleased! It is absurd to say that money is the root of all evil! The only way this could have been possible was for money to have existed in the beginning. Can you tell me where the money was located in the garden? Can you show me what verse in Genesis gives directions to the local bank? Money is not the root of all evil. The evil comes in to play when you value something - *something more than obeying God.*

But every man is tempted, when he is drawn away of his own lust, and enticed.

James 1:14

It is God's will for you to be prosperous! God created all wealth on this earth. He has set in place an economic system of prosperity. *You cannot receive God's financial abundance without obeying His financial plan!* To get started down the road to God's financial abundance you must accept the belief system that money is not evil, only loving it is. You must qualify for money by replacing your wrong information with right information...it is right to know that through your *obedience* you can receive from God what you need. Money is good when you do good things with it and it becomes a tool for you to use.

- **Money builds churches.**
- **Money feeds the hungry.**
- **Money evangelizes the world with the Gospel.**
- **Money produces Christian television and radio.**
- **Money feeds, clothes, and educates your family.**

If the devil can convince you to believe money is evil, that belief system will cause you to disrespect money and therefore keep you poor. *The devil doesn't want to destroy the Church; he wants to control it!* Without money, he keeps the Church from accomplishing God's final instruction... *"Go ye into all the world"!* The devil can't overcome or conquer God. However, if he can persuade you to believe a lie or myth about God's goodness, that lie will build a wall of doubt. To receive from God you must reach out by faith! *God does not respond to need; He only responds to faith.* Your doubt does not reach for God, but believes a lie.

God wants to give you His abundance, but can't unless you believe His Word. God's character will not allow Him to break one of His laws to fulfill another. Therefore, if you are not reaching by faith you are stumbling over doubt. God's Word clearly says... "*without faith it is impossible to please Him....*" When we do not embrace faith, the devil uses God's character against Him. Even though God wants to give to you, His character will not allow Him to break any of His laws. The only way to receive God's financial blessings is to believe by faith that He wants to give His very best to you. *Having money is not wrong, only loving it more than God is.* By the way, it was the *rich man*, Joseph of Arimathea, who supplied the tomb that Jesus was buried in. Imagine that! **A poor man couldn't have done this.**

Invest Your Time
Instead of
Spending It.

~~~

The Difference
Between
the Rich and Poor
Is How They Value
Their Time.

~ *Todd Coontz* ~

~~~

Myth #2

It Takes Money To Make Money

If you believe that it takes money to make money then chances are you will inventory your financial balance sheet and conclude with: *"I don't have enough money to invest in a project or make an investment; I can't make money without money."*

This belief system will cause you to feel hopeless about your present financial condition and will leave you believing that only a "miracle" from God would ever bring financial increase into your life. A "miracle" like Ed McMahon knocking at your door with a big fat check. A "miracle" like walking down the street and finding money that someone has lost. A "miracle" like your rich uncle dying and leaving you all his money. The "miracle" that tops them all – buying lottery tickets and believing you will win! *What you gain by a miracle you can lose through ignorance...***lack of relevant information!**

I believe in miracles! I have seen God do some extraordinary things in my life and in the lives of others. God can and still does perform miracles today! However, I also believe that God expects us to use the **talents, gifts,** and **abilities** that He has given us. The greatest of these gifts from God is *time*. It doesn't take money to make money. It takes *time* to make money. You trade your *time* for money. You work 40 hours a week for a paycheck. You have traded your time for money.

All of us have been given the same amount of *time* in a day. There are 60 seconds in a minute, 60 minutes in an hour, and 24 hours in a day. No matter how you calculate your *time*, whether by seconds, minutes, or even hours, it still adds up to the same mathematical solution for *time* in a day. The rich have not been given more *time* than the poor. The deciding difference between the amount of money that you have, compared to the amount of money that someone else has is *what you traded for your time.*

What Are You Trading Your Time For?

For example, you traded your time to watch a football game, and in return, you get the excitement of competition. You traded your time to nurture your family relationships, and in return, you have a family that loves you and children who know you. You traded your time to help the poor, and in return, you receive the satisfaction that you have given back to the less fortunate. You traded your time for television and school, and in return, you reaped what you watched and were taught. You traded your time to write a book, and in return, you are able to educate, encourage, and entertain people even after you're gone. You traded your time to read a book, and in return, you gained knowledge of a particular subject. During your lifetime you will trade your time for pleasure, fun, work, and even money. The question is, *"What are you trading your time for?"*

If you're lacking financially, it will always lead back to what you've traded your time for. Any Wealth Building course that does not address the subject of time management will not succeed, and I cannot emphasize this point enough! Here are four keys that will help you manage your time more wisely.

I. Establish Goals for Your Life

If we don't have a goal to get us from point A to point B, we will begin to mistake *"activity"* for *"accomplishment."* We will lower our expectations and dreams to match our incomes rather than expanding our incomes to match our dreams.

Mary Kay Ash, founder of Mary Kay Cosmetics, had a dream and set a goal in direct proportion to that dream. If she had set her goals based on her present income, her dream would have never been birthed into reality. Even after she became successful, every day she would write down six things to do that day and one by one, she would complete her tasks. ***Set financial goals based on your dreams*** and allow God to birth an idea for you to make sufficient money to accomplish your dreams. *Establish* your goals. *Write* them down. *List* them from the most important one to the least important one, and passionately accomplish them one by one. The *time* you trade to set goals will bring you a feeling of accomplishment and reward.

II. Establish Deadlines

When you establish deadlines don't only set them according to a task, but also for activities within a task. Don't spend an hour doing a 20 minute job. Something happens when you attach a deadline to a task or a dream! *Energy emerges* within you that you didn't even know you possessed!

III. Delegate If Possible

Spend your time being productive in the areas you're passionate about, have a gift for, or will produce your greatest financial reward. Keep in mind that there are other rewards for your time besides money. Because this book addresses the topic of money, we will limit our activities to the rewards that money will bring.

For instance, I love to mow grass. There is something about the smell of fresh cut grass that reminds me that every day is a new beginning. But, when I have more important and pressing things to do (like complete this book) I don't crank up the mower, I pay someone else to mow for me. You must always weigh the rewards and benefits of every task in your life. If you don't, the devil will make sure someone is there to rob your time from more important issues. You will then find yourself focusing on things less important. I call them ***time-robbers***. Who is robbing your time?

IV. Identify Your Best Energy Cycle

When are you at the highest level of energy during the day? Determine when that is and do the most difficult or mentally challenging tasks during this time. I own my own business, Coontz Investments, and I generally set my appointments first thing in the morning because I want to be at my best for my clients. Paperwork I will save for later in the day or will even delegate to someone else. It is difficult to work on "must be done today things" when your energy level is headed south. Also, make use of the latest time saving technologies that will help you to become more efficient and do the same tasks in less time. It will take some time to learn how to work them, but the future time saved will more than outweigh the time you initially invest. *Do not let other people's emergencies become your urgencies*. Highly productive and time conscious people assert their right to control their schedules based on more pressing tasks that must be completed.

Successful people are successful because they value their time. They realize on a daily basis that each moment is important, and they make sure every moment counts. You have been given the same amount of time as the rich. You will make the choice of what you will exchange your time for, how well you manage your time, and how much value you place on your time. This will determine your attitude towards completing your task. You attract what you respect, and what you don't respect will exit your life. Time is no exception! What you complete and what rewards you receive are based on how well and efficiently you manage your time. God has made available to you His riches and He desires to give them to you. **You must qualify to get what He has by doing what He says.** What will you trade your time for today?

Money Is Neither

Good Nor *Bad*.

~~~

It Only Makes

You More of

What You

Already Are.

~ *Todd Coontz* ~

~~~

Myth #3

Money Should Come to Me Because I Am A Good Person, And I Will Do Good Things With It

If being good was the only qualification for money then *why did Mother Teresa die broke?* Was she not a good person? Why are there thousands of good people in Africa dying because they have no money for food? What about all the innocent children in the world who have done no harm? Yet they suffer because they lack money. Wouldn't you agree with me that if being good was indeed the only qualification for money then there would be more who had it? I'm sure you can think of someone who is good and well deserving of money yet they are broke.

In contrast, being bad doesn't disqualify you from having money. If being bad excluded you from qualifying for money, then what happened on September 11, 2001, should have never happened. Think about what happened during Hitler's reign of terror and the six million plus Jews he killed unjustly. Think about all the evil people of this century who caused harm and destruction to mankind, all because they could afford to finance their evil deeds. Why? *Because being bad didn't disqualify them from money.*

I know by now you're saying to yourself, "You see, money *is* evil and having it *will* cause you to be bad and do bad things!" No, that's wrong! Being good doesn't qualify you for money and being bad doesn't disqualify you from having money. ***Money makes you more of what you already are.***

There is an underlying thought here concerning the belief system that some money is good and some money is bad. It's quite simple, but yet very profound. Money is neither good nor bad. Money is neutral. *Money takes on the personality and character of the person who is in control of it.* Money will move in the direction of the person who earns it ... good or bad. Money is not prejudiced toward race, religion, or sex. If you want some of it, or even if you want a lot of it, you must *qualify* for it.

When you qualify for money, you will become a magnet and money will gravitate towards you. Here are three Biblical Laws of Money and how you can qualify to receive it.

Law #1 — The Law of the Harvest

You qualify for money by your seed sowing and giving.

> *Give, and it shall be given unto you; good measure, pressed down, and shaken together, and running over, shall men give unto your bosom. For with the same measure that ye meet withal it shall be measured to you again.*
>
> *Luke 6:38*

But, remember this ... if you give a little, you will get a little. A farmer who plants just a few seeds will get only a small crop, but if he plants much, he will reap much.

2 Corinthians 9:6, TLB

Be not deceived; God is not mocked; for whatsoever a man soweth, that shall he also reap.

Galatians 6:7

The law of the harvest declares that before there can be a harvest a *seed* must first be sown. You cannot expect a harvest without first *sowing* a seed. Farmer Jones doesn't expect a harvest unless he knows that there were seeds sown into the ground. He knows that his only hope for survival is in the seed. There are four things that must happen before you get your harvest.

I. You Sow Your Seed Knowing That Every Seed Has an Invisible Instruction and Contains Life.

What is a seed? A **seed** is anything you can sow. *Time* is a seed. *Kindness* is a seed. *Love* is a seed. *Money* is a seed. Every seed has an invisible instruction that cannot be seen with the natural eye. Your seed is small. However, your seed is alive and contains an instruction to multiply and to reproduce after its kind. You sow corn to reap corn. You sow beans to reap beans. You sow apples to reap apples. You cannot see corn, beans, or apples when you sow the seed. However, you recognize that because of the invisible life contained in the seed, when the seed is sown, over time the evidence of life will emerge and your harvest will flourish. *Everything begins with a seed!*

II. You Sow Your Seed in Good Ground. It Is Just As Important Where You Sow As It Is What You Sow.

Every farmer spends time *qualifying* the soil. He wants to make sure that where he is sowing is good fertile ground. He will spend time preparing the soil, getting it ready for the seed. ***Note: The seed needs the ground more than the ground needs the seed!*** Make sure that the ground you're sowing in is good ground. You can determine if where you're sowing is good by asking yourself these questions: *Is it Biblical?* See what God's Word says about it. Has there been fruit in the past? Good ground always yields a good harvest! *Is there accountability both financially and spiritually?* What does your inner voice of the Holy Spirit tell you? You should have an inner peace about what you are doing. Remember, *Peace is Chief!*

III. You Sow Your Seed to the Harvest.

What do I mean by sowing to the harvest? If a farmer has a bad year, the following year he doesn't sow less seed, but he sows more seed to make up for the previous bad year. The farmer recognizes that he needs to make up for two years instead of one. He will do whatever he has to do to get more seeds, because he knows that he will never reap more from sowing less! You sow your seed in direct proportion to how much harvest you're expecting to receive. *If you have big needs you must sow many seeds!*

IV. You Sow in Faith and Wait Patiently.

But without faith it is impossible to please Him: for he that cometh to God must believe that He is, and that He is a rewarder of them that diligently seek Him.

Hebrews 11:6

...for whatsoever is not of faith is sin....
Romans 14:23

Four Wisdom Keys on Faith by Dr. Mike Murdock

1. "God's Only Pleasure Is to Be Believed, His Only Pain Is to Be Doubted."
2. "Your Seed Is a Photograph of Your Faith."
3. "The Seasons of Your Life Will Change Every Time You Decide to Use Your Faith."
4. "Seed-Faith Is Sowing What You Have Been Given to Create What You Have Been Promised."

You must wrap your faith around your seed and believe what God said about the laws of sowing and reaping! *Faith is rejecting our five senses and embracing hope.*

What follows sowing? Reaping, right? Wrong! The Bible talks about seed time *then* harvest. Seed ... Time ... Harvest. *Waiting* follows sowing. I have never seen a farmer yet sow one day and expect a harvest the next day. Have you? After you've sown your seed into good soil, you must wait patiently for your seed to germinate, take root, and eventually produce your harvest — *seed...time...harvest.*

Three Things I Will do With My Financial Harvest:

1. Give some away.
2. Save some for sowing again.
3. Save some for yourself.

When you do these three things you will place into motion what I call "momentum sowing." The *momentum* is similar to walking on a level escalator in an airport that carries you from one terminal to the other. As you walk the escalator moves too, your momentum builds up and your speed increases. You almost cover twice the ground in half the time. God doesn't always want you sowing from your needs or "must have a miracle today" circumstances. He wants to move you into the place where you're sowing from abundance. "Momentum sowing" is when you sow from the harvest you're presently enjoying to reap from the harvest that follows the next cycle. *Your seeds of today create your harvest of tomorrow!* You are continually sowing so that you stay in a perpetual season of harvest. This is what the Bible calls ABUNDANCE!

Law #2 — The Law of Wisdom

You qualify for money through your understanding. Knowledge is when you learn from your own mistakes. Wisdom is when you learn from the mistakes of others.

> *My people are destroyed for lack of knowledge: because thou hast rejected knowledge, I will also reject thee...*
>
> *Hosea 4:6*

> *Wisdom is the principal thing: therefore get wisdom: and with all thy getting get understanding.*
>
> *Proverbs 4:7*

You don't have a money problem; you have a wisdom problem! You cannot rise above your current level of understanding. To qualify for increase you must have more information. The wealthy know something that you don't know about money. They have the necessary information to help you qualify for the next level. ***Your information is the difference between your poverty or your prosperity! Your information is the difference between your success or your failure.*** What information are you lacking?

There Are Three Things You Can Do to Gain Wisdom and Understanding:

I. You Must Read Books About Money.

I can look at your library and predict your financial future. Information empowers you to do more and to be more. When you read, you are unlocking endless opportunities to explore through someone else's experiences things they have learned – usually through loss. *Experience is a good teacher, but it is also a tardy one.* Learn from the mistakes of others. When you buy a book about someone's life experiences you are saving yourself a lot of pain and grief, because it takes time to learn what they've already learned. Gain from their knowledge through the wonderful world of reading.

II. You Must Find a Financial Mentor.

Do you have a financial advisor? Do you have a good CPA? How about a good attorney? The wealthy do! Seek out those individuals who are experts in their fields and use them. Surround yourself with people who are financially successful and ask them questions. They know something you don't know.

III. You Must Change Your Financial Habits.

We are not creatures of discipline but creatures of habit. People who are successful financially have created good habits. Change your habits and your financial future will change too. To change your habits you must first acknowledge that your way of thinking is incorrect. *You cannot outperform your knowledge!*

Here Are Four Good Financial Habits to Practice:

1. Spend less than you make.
2. Save at least 10 percent of what you make and save it consistently.
3. Save money in tax-deductible and tax-deferred investments.
4. Never borrow what you don't have the money to pay for.

Law #3 — The Law of the Talents

You qualify for money by using the talents you have been given.

> *And unto one he gave five talents, to another two, and to another one; to every man according to his several ability; and straitway took his journey.*
>
> *Matthew 25:15*

The law of the talents says that you must use what the Lord has given you, putting your talents to work and building on it. I believe that everyone has been given talents by God. It is our responsibility to discover them and build on what we've been given.

Three Clues to Discovering Your Talents

I. You Discover Your Talents by What You Love.

What do you love to do? What excites you the most? What would you do for free? Love is a powerful emotion. The Bible says that all else may fail but love will never fail. Tiger Woods loves golf. Jeff Gordon loves racing. Thomas Kinkade loves to paint. Donald Trump loves real estate. Bill Gates loves computers. Your love is a good indication of something you can be passionate about. Passionate people will always excel to higher levels of excellence. Your level of excellence will cause you to stand out from the crowd and you will be rewarded accordingly. **Your discovery of your passion will guarantee your financial rewards.**

II. You Discover Your Talents by What You Hate.

What do you hate? Your anger can motivate you to take action against what you hate. *I hate poverty!* I'm writing this book because I want the myths about money to be dispelled and I want the truth to be told. My hatred for poverty motivates me and keeps me traveling thousands of miles and scheduling hundreds of appointments each year. I want to help people fulfill their dreams by solving their financial problems. Your financial increase is determined by your discovery that there are problems waiting to be solved, and that you will be rewarded for the solutions you provide. The kinds of problems you solve will determine the size of your financial reward. You will pay a computer consultant $75.00 an hour and pay a maid only $15.00 an hour. If you are not making enough money, then solve more difficult problems. Find problems that few people are willing to put forth the effort to prepare and study for. Become an Uncommon Problem Solver! *What you hate will determine what you are willing to attack.* Discover and hate only the right things.

III. You Discover Your Talents by What Comes Natural.

This discovery is perhaps the most important of them all. It is possible to love something and be horrible at it. America's favorite sport is said to be baseball. I know a lot of people who are in love with the game. Some even grew up believing that someday they would be in the Major League. So even though your love for something is there, it doesn't guarantee you are any good at it.

Look at the life of Michael Jordan. Put a basketball in his hands and he can be matched by few. He glides through the air with such grace that it appears as though he has just taken flight and is suspended in midair. He is arguably the greatest basketball player who has ever lived. Michael loves the game of basketball and it comes natural to him. He loves baseball as well. Michael worked very hard to become a great baseball player; although he was willing to make sacrifices to achieve his goal, it did not appear he had the same natural talent for baseball that he did for basketball. Michael Jordan also has a love for golf. Although he is better than most people who set out to play the game, he is certainly no Tiger Woods. Michael Jordan is a great athlete. It has been incredible to see him achieve a level of excellence in both baseball and golf, but basketball came more natural to him than any other sport he played.

What comes natural to you is a good indication of something you are gifted to do. Love or hate is not enough to guarantee you'll make money at it. But, couple them with your natural talents and your possibilities of financial rewards have just increased substantially. Pause for a moment and think about what you may have neglected to recognize. Dr. Mike Murdock has an incredible book entitled *The Law of Recognition.* The book has these phrases in it: "*What is not recognized will not be celebrated. What is not celebrated will go unrewarded.* ***What goes unrewarded will exit your life***." I want to encourage you to purchase this book from the Wisdom Center, P.O. Box 99, Denton, Texas. **When you discover your talent, your rewards will be uncovered!**

Three Actions I Will Take Towards Changing My Mentality

1. ____

____

____

____

____

2. ____

____

____

____

____

____

3. ____

____

____

____

What You Have
Can Be Stolen
From You.

~~~

What You Are
Can Never
Be Taken Away.

~ *Todd Coontz* ~

~~~

Myth #4

When I Get More Money Then I Will Give and Save

How many times have you heard someone say, "When I get more money I will give?" If I had a nickel for every time I've heard that statement, then I would have more money myself to give. How about you? Have you ever uttered that statement from your lips?

I'm the owner of Coontz Investments & Insurance, Inc., a financial services firm. I've enjoyed helping clients achieve their dreams for over a decade and I love it. I have people come to me all the time and say, "Todd, when I get a lot of money then I will come see you so you can help me invest it." Guess what? Most of the people who make that statement will never come to see me with money. Why? Because they don't understand money and how it really works. If they understood money, they would know that you always start with what you already have. *Oak trees always begin first as a tiny seed.*

Seven Myths About Money is more than just another book talking about how you can get rich. The message of prosperity that Jesus taught always addressed your character first. He taught that who you are and what you love was more important than what you possess. *What you have can be stolen from you, but what you are can never be taken away*!

You will learn that money is really an extension of what you are, and what you are matters more than what you have. However, you can be good and have money too! Money is only a tool. Have you ever heard the phrase "You are what you eat"? *You are what you believe as well!* What myth do you believe today?

I've recently heard that the average person who wins the lottery is broke within 18 to 24 months after receiving their million dollar winnings. Why? How could this be possible? There is another saying that goes something like this: *"Fools and money will soon part."* Remember, getting the money is just the beginning; keeping it is harder!

The only way that money will remain in your life is if you have the mentality that gives money the permission to stay. People who receive large sums of money at once hardly ever have the mentality or expertise to keep it. Your understanding about money will determine whether you keep it or lose it. It's your choice.

Look at Matthew, chapter 25, verses 14-29. I believe what Jesus taught His disciples about money is important to note here. He illustrates, by using this parable, three principles that are invaluable to your financial success. It deals with the actions taken by three servants who each had an opportunity to multiply what they were given. Two of the servants were found to be good and faithful stewards, and one was a wicked and slothful servant. The difference between the good and the wicked servants was their belief system. Each of them had the same opportunity, but only two seized it. The parable describes their belief on how money was earned, multiplied, and how they viewed their master.

Their belief system dictated their actions and decided their future. *You cannot move beyond what you really believe!* I challenge you to examine what you believe about money and learn from these three servants. You will learn: 1) The Principle of Stewardship; 2) The Principle of Beginnings; and 3) The Principle of Faithfulness.

The Principle of Stewardship...What We Possess Is Really God's Gifts Given to Us for Use.

For the kingdom of heaven is as a man traveling into a far country, who called his own servants, and delivered unto them his goods.

Matthew 25:14

We must never forget where our blessings really come from! We are living in a society that continuously declares, "It's mine, all mine. I've earned it by myself!" Everywhere you look you see self-sufficiency and self-will. Hardly anybody wants to share the credit for their success with others.

Remember, no one gets to the top without help from others. People are always a key ingredient to your success. Always recognize that your success has been possible because of the people you surround yourself with. Give them credit too.

Rewards of Stewardship

We must recognize that what we've received are gifts to us and we are stewards of these gifts, not owners. *Stewardship is rewarding.* You see, if you are an owner, then it's your primary responsibility to pay all the expenses that goes along with maintaining and taking care of something. But as a steward you have access to these things without the expense. Sound like a great idea? It is.

Here's a great example to illustrate my point. There was an old television show in the early eighties called *Magnum P.I.*

Magnum owned nothing. In fact, he owed money to most of his closest friends. Even though he was penniless and broke, that didn't stop him from living the "good life." He lived in Hawaii on an estate just off the ocean where he would take frequent swims. He drove around in a red Ferrari, not to mention the other vehicles he had access to. It didn't cost him a dime! It was the owner's responsibility to pay the expenses necessary to keep these things up, the owner being Robin Masters.

Recognize the Difference Between Owners and Stewards

Stewards oversee what belongs to someone else; in return, they have the privilege of its use. Owners, on the other hand, have title right given by law, but they also incur the expenses. God has granted us access to all that is His. It is our job to oversee what we've received from Him. He will provide what is necessary to cover the expenses for what He's given to us. To *qualify* for God's supply we must be stewards, not owners.

How do you know whether you're an owner or steward? Easy, by your willingness to surrender to His request. If God asked you to give your money, would you be willing to release it? Without hesitation? If you find yourself making excuses as to why you should keep it, you're an owner. If I handed you $100 and requested that you hold it for me, when I asked you for it would you argue with me giving me five reasons why you should keep it? Absolutely not! It wouldn't even cross your mind. Why? Because the $100 was entrusted to you to hold, not to keep. When you're willing to walk away from something that is valuable to you because God requested you to, He knows that you value His instructions and wisdom. *Obedience* is proof that you're a steward and not an owner.

I don't want to be an owner. I choose to be a steward and I will recognize where my blessings come from. *God will give you as much as He can trust you with.* How much are you being trusted?

We Must Manage These Gifts Well

How well you manage these gifts will determine whether you can be trusted with more. **Increase is the reward you receive as a result of the care you give to what has been entrusted to you.** God wants to get money to you, but cannot until He can get money *through* you! You should be like a conduit allowing His blessings to flow through you for His good work. You must be diligent and multiply what you've been given if you expect to receive more. This parable teaches you about a man who divided his talents (money) among his three servants. He gave five, two and even one talent. Two servants multiplied their talents, even doubled them. However, the servant with one talent hid it in the earth out of fear.

> *...Lord, I knew thee that thou art a hard man, reaping where thou hast not sown, and gathering where thou hast not strewed.*
>
> *Matthew 25:24*

This servant had what I call a poverty mentality charged by fear. What is a *"poverty mentality"?* It is when you believe that somebody else owes you something that you didn't earn, and you think that you deserve it just because of your existence. It also causes you to believe that the person you're receiving it from hasn't earned it either (reaping where thou hast not sown, or gathering where thou hast not strewed). If this is what you believe then you have a poverty mentality.

The only gift we cannot earn is salvation! Jesus paid that price for us and it is freely given to all who will accept it. There still remains a Biblical system designed by principles governing your financial prosperity. You will not receive increase without first obeying the instructions regarding these principles on the subject of money. *The world has embraced His principles while rejecting the person of Jesus. The Church has embraced the person of Jesus, while rejecting His principles.* The world receives the rewards of His principles while rejecting His salvation. The Church receives His salvation while rejecting the rewards of His principles. Knowing Him is only the beginning. You must allow Him to do a completed work in you. *You must follow His financial principles to receive His financial rewards.*

Gifts and talents are really God's deposits in our personal accounts, but we determine the interest on them. The greater the amount of hard work and attention we give to them, the greater the value becomes. His gifts are never loans; they are deposits. It's our responsibility to bring Him a good return and we must develop our talents and gifts so that dividends can be paid. Don't allow a *poverty mentality* to rob you of what has been given to you through Biblical principles.

Being broke requires no faith. It requires only fear. To qualify for a life of nothing requires you to do nothing except be lazy. *Prosperity demands your* ***faith****, your* ***obedience****, and a lot of* ***hard work!*** Thomas Edison once said, "Most people never recognize an opportunity because it usually comes dressed in bib overalls and always requires work." Have you really qualified for increase?

The Principle of Beginnings... Everything Begins Small.

And unto one have given five talents, to another two, and to another one; to every man according to his several ability; and straightway took his journey.
Matthew 25:15

Everything has a beginning. Massive skyscrapers begin first with one steel beam. Homes are constructed by using two by fours one at a time. Foundations are dug before they are poured. Sowing always precedes reaping. Babies crawl before they can walk. You must walk before you can run. Books begin with the first chapter. There cannot be an ending before there's a beginning. Everything has a beginning!

God always has a *progression of pattern*. He is *ceremonial* and *ritualistic*. There is always a time and a season for God's system and His financial rewards. When you understand this principle you will not scoff at your present beginnings, no matter how small they may be.

For who hath despised the day of small things?...
Zechariah 4:10

Most of my clients that are millionaires started saving with their first dollar. They set aside every week a little out of each paycheck consistently week after week. Time and compounding interest multiplied their money resulting in millionaire status over a 30-year period.

Consider an 18-year-old who saves as little as $30 each month or $1.00 a day. If he consistently earns 12% each year tax-deferred until the age of 65, his money would have grown to over a million dollars. Warren Buffet, the billionaire investor, once said, "The habit of setting aside a little from each paycheck is more important than how much." He knows that good habits will create wealth. People decide their habits;, their habits decide their future. Have you created good habits of prosperity? *You must begin with your first dollar.*

Every farmer knows that there will never be a harvest without first beginning with those tiny seeds. I have never heard of a farmer who wanted a harvest say, "I don't have much so I won't sow anything this year." He would never say something as ridiculous as that, because he understands the laws that govern the harvest. The farmer knows that he must start with what he already has, and when he sows his seeds, they will multiply and produce a generous harvest. Inventory what you have now. Don't think about all the things you need or do not presently have. *As long as you inventory what you don't have you will never receive what you need!* Sow from what you possess today. A farmer fully understands that he must sow in order to qualify for reaping. The myth: When I get more money, then I will give and save. That's really what it is — a myth.

The Principle of Faithfulness...
Remain Constant to Your Assignment.

His Lord said unto him, Well done, thou good and faithful servant; thou hast been faithful over a few things, I will make thee ruler over many things: enter thou into the joy of the Lord.

Matthew 25:23

What does it mean to be faithful? **Faith is rejecting our senses for the sake of hope!** The trying of your faith produces a stronger and deeper faith. To receive the reward of faithfulness you must remain faithful during times of severe testing. Any successful person will testify that the reason they're successful is that they never gave up.

A wicked messenger falleth into mischief; but a faithful ambassador is health.

Proverbs 13:17

There will always be opportunities to take the road less traveled. Distractions will be placed in front of you trying to get you off course. Resist them all! Remain faithful to your assignment and financial rewards will gravitate in your direction. God always rewards faithfulness! Be patient. Recognize that to everything there is a time and season. Your time will come, and when it does it will bring you joy.

You will learn that you are a steward over what God has entrusted in your hands. Acknowledge that everything has a beginning and usually starts very small; and whatever your assignment may be, remain *faithful* to it and do it with all of your heart. This myth, *When I get more money then I will give and save,* will not have any hold on your mentality. You will be well on your way to financial abundance based on God's provision provided by His principles for success!

Your Mentality
Determines
Your Wealth.

~~~

You Must
Respect Money
to Attract Money.

~ *Todd Coontz* ~

~~~

Myth #5

I Have to Become A Rat to Win the Rat Race

In the world today we refer to the hustle and bustle of everyday life as being a rat race! Everybody is in a hurry and it seems that nobody has any time left to *offer* a helping hand. *Life* has become a race. Really, you don't even have a choice whether or not to participate. *Living automatically enters you into the race!* However, you can decide and make choices on how you will think, act, and respond to those around you.

An Underlying Belief System That Is Founded on Half-Truth

There is an *underlying belief system* in the world today that believes the rich have received their money because they **lied, cheated,** or **inherited** it. It has found its way into the hearts and minds of almost every person in the world today. This belief has been taught and passed down for generations supported by inaccurate information and at best founded upon *half-truth.*

This belief will create a conflict for you and your desire to accumulate wealth. While you are working toward your financial goals, your **subconscious** mind will tell you that to succeed you must become dishonest. You cannot move beyond your thought life. *What you believe will determine how you act.* Now the conflict begins. On one hand you want money, on the other hand you want to be honest. You are faced with a decision. What will you decide? You won't. Your belief system will! The end result will be that the rich will get richer, and the poor will get poorer! Why? Your belief system determines your actions. *Your mentality links poverty with honesty and prosperity with dishonesty!* You therefore buy into the myth "I have to become a *rat* to win the *rat race*," a *rat* being somebody that is shady and dishonest, thus creating the conflict.

There Has Always Been Some Kind of Conflict

Today, we recognize that there still exists a conflict between people of **gender, race,** and **religion.** We have made enormous strides to bridge the gap so that every person is treated equally based on their qualifications. We are not biased toward their religious beliefs, the color of their skin, or whether they are male or female. We should never cease from our efforts until everyone has that God-given right of equality.

Nothing ever comes without cost or sacrifice. Tremendous sacrifices by great men and women have been made because they believed in a cause that was bigger than they were. They were willing to make tough decisions and give their all to the cause they so fervently fought for. People like the great Protestant Reformer *Martin Luther,* who, through his strong convictions concerning salvation through grace alone, was instrumental in breaking down religious barriers that existed for centuries. People like *Susan B. Anthony,* who fought for the women's right to vote. Through her sacrifice and relentless efforts, all over America today women have the right to cast their votes in ballot boxes during each election.

In the year 1966, in Washington, DC, an African-American preacher named *Martin Luther King, Jr.,* delivered a speech that would forever change the racial fabric of America. As he stood at the Washington Memorial and delivered the speech *I Have a Dream,* he declared that he looked for the day when men would be judged by **"the character of their heart, not the color of their skin."** He fought for the equality between the races, which was very controversial and unpopular at the time. It cost him his life.

The Fight for Equality Among Financial Classes

As humanity continues the fight for equality among religions, genders, and races there still remains a conflict that is rarely ever addressed. It is a conflict that has existed for thousands of years. Unlike other conflicts there is an ever-widening gap that seems to increase with time. This gap is among the financial classes of people.

Even though there are about four financial classes based upon the current progressive tax brackets, there are really only two. These two classes are a reality because of how they are perceived by the other class. I am referring to the classes of the *"haves"* and the *"have nots."*

Money Is Relative

Money *is* relative. You require a certain amount of money to accomplish your dreams, while somebody else needs a different amount. What you think is an enormous sum of money could be pocket change to another. Therefore, your pocket change may even be more than what someone else requires. My financial dreams and goals are different than Donald Trump's financial dreams and goals. Money's *relativity* is based on your financial needs, goals and dreams.

Words Are Windows, Walls, or Doorways

I want to take a moment to point out a very important truth: *Words* matter. Words become windows, walls, or doorways. *They are your entrance into your future and they are your exit from your past*. Knowing the meanings of the words you use also matters. There is a branch of linguistics called *semantics* which can be defined as the study dealing with the nature of language. Semanticists emphasize a point that seems like an obvious truth: *You think with words*. If you think with words then it is important to know the meaning of the words you use. Otherwise, you cannot think clearly. For example, when a millionaire thinks of *wealth* does he have the same kind of mental image, the same definition that a homeless person or that single mother on welfare might have? The very meaning of the word *wealth* depends on the user's mental picture based on his prejudices, hopes and even fears. This thought also applies to the words *money* and *prosperity*.

Before you can think clearly and deeply about any subject you must first have some experience with it. The more experience you have, generally speaking, the more reliable your judgment will be. This experience can be gained in four ways: (1) by personal observation; (2) by listening; (3) by mentorship; and (4) by reading. When a financial advisor states his opinion about your current financial future his judgment is likely to be highly reliable because his experience with the subject matter is broad. But when the same financial advisor is asked to give his opinion about why your car won't start his judgment will be less reliable than your mechanic's. *Experience is the essential difference.*

What Is a Myth?

The definition of a myth is a belief statement that is not accurate or completely true. It usually contains an element of truth, but also just enough falsehood to be dangerous. However, if you don't realize that a myth is false and you act on what you have been taught...even though it's false it can harm you. *You cannot believe wrong information and get right results*! There is a reason why the gap between the *"haves"* and the *"have nots"* is widening. I have spent the past twelve years of my life studying the subject of money. I wanted to learn why there was such a wide gap between the classes. I have studied the rich and their habits. I have taken classes on money and wealth management. I have observed them both professionally and personally. I have discovered through my reading, interviewing, consulting, observing, and asking questions that the common denominator of the two classes is simply how they *think* and what they *think* about.

The Wealthy Are Typically Honest

Recently I read a book entitled *The Millionaire Mind* written by Thomas J. Stanley, Ph.D. He conducted a survey of 733 millionaires who were asked to rate thirty success factors. Here are the top seven:

Seven Things You Will Do to Change Your Mentality

1. **Being honest with all people.**
2. **Being well disciplined.**
3. **Getting along with people.**
4. **Having a supportive spouse.**
5. **Working harder than most people.**
6. **Loving my career/business.**
7. **Having strong leadership qualities.**

Wealthy people are not typically shady or dishonest. They have a strong belief in doing what is right. However, most people believe that they are dishonest. This belief is not reality! The nicest people I have met are people with money.

My family and I recently moved into a new house in the wealthiest subdivision in my city. It is a gated community and inside the subdivision we live in the Estate Section, where homes range from $500,000 to upwards of over a million dollars. To compare: the average home in my city sells for about $150,000 dollars. When we moved in, our neighbors whom we had never met brought us pies, cakes, and flowers as housewarming gifts welcoming us to the neighborhood. I can't ever remember this kind of hospitality in our old subdivision, where we lived for over seven years.

What Is Prosperity?

I want to stop here for a moment and define what I believe real prosperity is. *Prosperity is having more than enough to accomplish God's instructions for you.*

The subject of prosperity, we have recently learned, has different meanings to different people. The meanings are derived from our personal experiences based on the hand that has been dealt to us by life. However, God has dealt another hand, and He holds all the cards. He is willing to shuffle them in your favor.

Here are four Wealth Keys that will help you change your mentality....*your mentality determines your prosperity.*

I. Your Character Determines Your Prosperity

What you are matters more than what you have. The prosperity message that Jesus taught was more significant than what you achieve during your lifetime. He always addressed the heart of the person along with their character. Your character is important. In fact, we've heard of the saying "The road to hell is paved with good intentions."

> *"Your good intentions do not decide your future... your character does."*
>
> *– Todd Coontz*

II. Your Work Ethic Determines Your Prosperity

I learned this from my father. He probably was the hardest working man I've ever met. He worked all the time, but yet always made time for his family. Today my work ethic is much the same. It's easy for me to work because of the example my father set. I think a vital key to financial success is to have a work ethic that demands that you will not quit until you complete each task. The wealthy people I've observed and questioned have an incredible work ethic that is second to none. Make no mistake about it, they believe in working hard. I asked God once, "Why do so many religious people fight the message of prosperity?" He simply said to me, "Todd, it requires no faith to be poor." To receive what you need from God, the formula is *faith coupled with action.* I believe that anyone, no matter what color of skin you have, no matter what gender, no matter what side of the tracks you were born on, through faith and belief in the principles taught in the Bible...you can achieve prosperity. *You can do it!*

III. Your Pursuit of Your Dreams Determines Your Prosperity

All of us have dreams. Through each conflict we have faced over time, this country has been shaped and forged by *dreamers.* Successful people are people who dream. They are willing to pursue their dreams, even if it means a level of risk that is uncomfortable. There are no guarantees in life. To everything, there is always some level of risk, and everything requires some level of faith. The questions remain, "What will you have faith in?" and "How much risk are you willing to assume?" Millionaires dream big and sometimes even lose big. Always calculate and measure how much risk you are willing to assume. *Don't ever let anyone steal your dreams.*

IV. Your Realistic Expectations Determines Your Prosperity

Not everyone will achieve millionaire status. You may never be rich like Bill Gates or Sam Walton, or even Donald Trump. They have accomplished what few people are capable of doing. They have been given rare opportunities and have seized those opportunities to achieve incredible wealth. Their wealth has not been *inherited*... it has truly been **created.** They have learned and applied many of the principles I have shared in this book. There is still hope for you! I believe everyone has within them the seed of greatness! You have been created in the image of God, and after His likeness. God will provide you with every opportunity to reach your level of prosperity, so you will *accomplish* each instruction that He will give you. If you will apply the principles taught in this book, while still remaining patient... you too can succeed. *You will succeed if you will believe.*

Three Financial Goals I Will Accomplish in the Next 12 Months

1. ____

____

____

____

____

2. ____

____

____

____

____

____

3. ____

____

____

____

The Borrower
Is Always
the Servant
to the Lender.

~~~

A Lifestyle of
Debt
Creates A Lifetime of
Pain.

~ *Todd Coontz* ~

~~~

Myth #6

I Must Borrow Money To Buy the Things I Want

The American Bankers Association in Washington, DC, has reported that bankruptcies total more than $1 million a year for the first time ever. Compared to only a decade ago, personal bankruptcies have *doubled.*

Why is there such an alarming number of financial catastrophes? Because consumers are carrying a burden of credit card debt that reached a record high in 1996. Principal and interest payments account for 11 cents of every dollar Americans earn after taxes. Home mortgage interest payments and debt service consume a record high of 17 percent of personal disposable income, up from 15.5 percent in 1993.

Credit Card Debt

The typical American adult has nine credit cards and average balances totaling almost $4,000. Banks send out 2.7 billion credit card solicitations a year or 17 for each person between the ages of 18 and 65. Credit has become so easy to obtain, and is causing consumers to overspend on items they can't afford. When did you receive your last credit card *solicitation?*

The Wealth Effect

Add to the equation the recent bull market of the late nineties, which has caused what Federal Reserve Chairman Allen Greenspan referred to as *"the wealth effect."* This was based on stock prices with high PE (price to earnings ratios). Simply put, inflated stock prices based on increased speculation of projected growth of the economy, instead of growth that is more realistic. This has left the average consumer with a false feeling of prosperity. Consumers have been relying on numbers that are projected based on the hope that the economy will remain red-hot! For instance, in order to keep up with these projected numbers, the economy would have to maintain a growth rate that would be similar to Jeff Gordon racing his car through downtown Dallas, Texas, without stopping at any of the red lights and causing a catastrophe. *Possible?* Yes. Likely? **No.**

The Effect of Unrealistic Projections

The average consumer has based their financial budgets on inflated stock prices supported by unrealistic projections. This is affecting consumers because they are now adjusting their spending habits based on the hope of future pay raises. This has caused a mentality of "charge now and pay later." This mind-set places the emphasis on the question "How much are the monthly payments?" instead of "Can I really afford this?" Sound familiar?

Real prosperity doesn't assume anything. It's not presumptuous. It is not financed with someone else's money who, in return, charges you an interest rate for allowing you to use their money. True prosperity is net worth (assets minus liabilities) driven instead of debt finance.

In a Recession

Today, March 18, 2002, as I sit here in my study we are currently suffering from a recession in America. The stock market has given back (gone down) the enormous gains in the last couple of years. The billion dollar energy company, Enron, is collapsing because of bad accounting practices, leaving many employees broke and without a job. The majority of companies are reporting lower than expected returns on earnings. This is because consumer spending is way down, leaving the average company with an over-supply of inventory. *Every economy operates on the principle of supply and demand.* When there is more supply of products than there is demand for products, it causes the economy to contract (pull back). This happens because companies stop the wheels of production, causing the demand for more employees to stop. Companies now have a build-up of inventory which nobody needs now. This results in a much *slower* growth rate than was projected by economists. Consumers, who were depending on raises to finance their dreams, are realizing that they are probably not going to get their raises. Really, the average company is forced to stop giving raises in order to survive. Consumers are now left with debt ratios that are too high and without the possibilities of raises…no more money to pay these debts off! In addition, there has been political uncertainty on foreign soil. Yet, while Americans are facing these difficult financial times, they are forced to cope with the memory of September 11, 2001. This tragedy has left thousands of Americans without their family and friends.

A Better System

The world's economic condition may be in distress today. Even if your financial expectations, depending on the world's system, have left you in a financial mess, there is hope… *God has a way — a better system.* The Church should be offering solutions to the world and seizing the opportunity to evangelize. Sadly, the Church isn't really any better off financially than the world because they too have depended on the world's system. The myth *"I Must Borrow Money to Buy the Things I Want"* has created a mentality in the Church that places faith in an economic system that does not offer God's very best way. A system that is presumptuous! The Bible is very clear concerning the requirements necessary to receive what we need from God ... it's called *faith.*

> *But without faith it is impossible to please Him ...*
> *Hebrews 11:6*

The majority of the modern-day churches have accepted Christ as their Savior, while *rejecting His principles concerning money.* All of us have faith. The question is not "Do I have faith?" but rather "What do I have faith in?"

Many churches have placed their faith in the world's system instead of the principles that Jesus taught. Most have a mortgage on their buildings, which proves my point. This is so wrong because Christians that pay their tithes to the local church are also paying interest to the bank. That's how the bank makes money. This is so tragic because the interest paid to the bank gives the Church less to promote and evangelize the world, which is the *"Great Commission."* Do I want you to quit paying your tithes? **Absolutely not!** However, I do want you to recognize that there is a better way and I want to encourage you to believe God to help you pay off your church mortgage while freeing up extra capital for His work. When you trust the principles and laws taught in the Bible, you are acknowledging that God is your source.

The World's System Encourages Debt

The world's system encourages *debt* rather than *ownership.* The crash of 1933 was the result of banks collapsing due to consumers being unable to service their debt obligations on their farms and businesses. This caused a steep decline in the stock market, and investors who had margin accounts were receiving *"margin calls"* on their accounts. A margin account is when you *"borrow"* the money from a brokerage firm to buy more stock. The brokerage firm will *"loan"* you the money and charge you an *"interest rate."* The problem in 1933 was that there were no *"limits"* on how much you could borrow against your stocks. It was possible to buy a stock on *"margin"* and watch it go down in value, yet still owe the brokerage firm the *"interest"* and the money *"loaned"* against the purchase of the stock. Many investors *"leveraged"* their stocks to buy more stocks, hoping that the rise in the market would give them enough gain for a profit, along with the ability to pay back the brokerage firm the money they *"borrowed."* Well, I do not need to tell you what happened. ***Please take note: Today there are "limits" on how much you can "borrow" on margin.*** This system financed by debt is not God's best financial plan for you! The Bible teaches us to be owners and strongly cautions us to understand that the borrower is servant to the lender.

> *The rich ruleth over the poor, and the borrower is servant to the lender.*
>
> *Proverbs 22:7*

It Is Not Wrong to Borrow

It's not wrong to borrow. I do not believe in never borrowing. In a time of need, *a properly handled loan can serve you well.* However, you must adopt a *belief system* that only allows you to borrow for appreciable assets. *What would be considered an appreciable asset?* Your home, because you need some place to live, and it's typically cheaper to own than to rent. Your car, only because you need dependable transportation to get to work so you can earn a living. Anything that appreciates in value or has a correlating asset could be a candidate for a loan. Clothes, vacations, leisure items and things of that sort would be considered a liability. *What is a liability?* Something that costs you more money to own than you could ever get in return if you needed to sell it. *Whether you have liabilities or assets, it is important to make sure that you have adequate income and sufficient cash reserves in case of a downturn in the economy.*

Borrowing Should Not Be a Lifestyle

The point that I want to emphasize here is that borrowing should not be a lifestyle. There are circumstances where borrowing money may be permissible. However, you must be *cautious* not to allow *debt* to become a way of life for you and your family. I have written this book because I want to help you change your *mentality* on how you view debt. I believe that you must *change* your *belief system* about debt in order to be free from the "*spirit of debt.*" The purpose of this book is to educate you and help you exchange wrong information with corrected information. God does not want you or your family under the control or the burden of debt! Here are three principles that I believe will help you *change* your "*mentality of debt.*" You must decide: 1) I will not make debt a lifestyle. 2) I will adopt a good confession. 3) God will empower me to get out of debt when I change my mind.

I. I Will Not Make Debt a Lifestyle

You are empowered by the choices you make. Decide today that you will make wise choices. First of all, decide to destroy all your credit cards! Keep only the ones you need for convenience. If you do not have the money to purchase something…wait until God provides it. Second of all, your mentality will begin to change when you establish different habits…so create good financial habits. And last, carry cash with you to purchase items. You will discover that you will become more careful about what you spend your hard-earned money on.

II. I Will Adopt a Good Confession

> ***Death and life*** *are in the power of the tongue: and they that love it shall eat the fruit thereof.*
>
> *Proverbs 18:21*

Words matter. I remember one day when Dr. Mike Murdock and I were talking about this very subject. He said something to me that I will never forget. He said, *"Todd, what you say matters, but what they remember matters more."* Dr. Murdock even took this scriptural principle to an even higher level. What you say matters, but how you say it is just as important. Listen to what King Solomon had to say about being careful what you say.

> *Thou art snared with the* ***words*** *of thy mouth; thou art taken with the* ***words*** *of thy mouth.*
>
> *Proverbs 6:2*

The words you speak and the confession you make matters. *Your words will change the climate of your financial crisis!* If you really want to supercharge your mind-set…*speak to your circumstances*. Boldly begin to say, "Abundance is provided for me by God's Word!" You should say, "I will not have a mentality or lifestyle of debt!" Speak to your mountain of debt. **God gave you a mouth to conquer your mind.**

> *For verily I say unto you, That whosever shall say unto the mountain, Be thou removed, and be thou cast into the sea; and shall not doubt in his heart, but shall*

believe that those things which he saith shall come to pass; he shall have whatsoever he saith.

Mark 11:23

Trash Talk

Let me give you an example to illustrate what I am saying. In the game of basketball, the players have what they call *"trash talk."* During the game the players will speak negative *words* to their opponents throughout the entire game. For example, "My grandmother has more game than you do!" or maybe, "You need to be on the injured list!" Truthfully, it can even get more evasive and harsher than this. The point being, the players recognize the *words* they speak are powerful. Their *words* will help them defeat their opponents. *Your wealth is found in your mouth!*

Faith... Supercharges Your Words

Another key ingredient necessary to supercharge your words is...*your faith*. Remember, power comes only when you believe the thing you are saying will actually come to pass.

*...and shall not **doubt** in his heart, but shall **believe**...*

Mark 11:23

The Bible teaches us the words we speak and believe are powerful! Faith-filled words have the power to change your impossible circumstances into *"miracle solutions"!* I really don't believe that we fully appreciate the power we possess by our ***faith-filled spoken words***. Please take note: God created the world by His spoken Word.

And God said:

Let there be light: and there was light…

Let there be a firmament in the midst of the waters and let it divide the waters from the waters…

Let the waters under the heavens be gathered together in one place and let the dry land appear…

And it was so.

From Genesis 1:3, 6-7, 9

Do Not Be Double-Minded

When you are *double-minded* your words become powerless. Listen to what James says…

> *…let him ask in faith, nothing wavering. For he that wavereth is like a wave of the sea driven with the wind.*
>
> *James 1:6*

When you are *double-minded* you will say one thing with your mouth while believing another thing with your heart…or vice versa. Your confession should line up with what is in your heart. In fact, the Bible teaches that your heart will tell on you.

> *…for out of the abundance of the heart the mouth speaketh.*
>
> *Matthew 12:34*

The real prosperity message the Bible teaches deals with the *hearts* of fallen humanity. *What you are is more important than what you have.* However, when God changes your heart, what you are also changes. Search the Scriptures diligently. Discover what God says about each circumstance you may face. He will provide you with solutions concerning every question that you will ever ask. When you surrender your thoughts for His thoughts, and your ways for His ways, your spoken *words* will be consistent with His desire for your life. *You will not be double-minded, but God-minded!*

Testimony Is Powerful

Document on paper every battle that you have fought in the past. Journal every victory that God has given you! Share with others every miracle you have received. Recall the memories of your mind in the corridors of your heart. All of the victories you have received and all of the enemies you have conquered will remind you of God's mighty power. Your testimony is perhaps the most powerful weapon you possess in your arsenal! *God wants to turn your memories of the past into your hope for the future!*

> *And they overcame him (devil) by the word of their testimony.*
>
> *Revelation 12:11*

III. God Will Empower Me

God will never require you to do anything without first equipping you to complete each task. God promises to provide for you sufficient grace and strength to accomplish His will for your life. Remember, it is God that gives to you the power to get wealth.

> *...Remember the Lord thy God: for it is He that giveth thee power to get wealth, that He may establish His covenant which He sware unto thy fathers, as it is this day.*
>
> *Deuteronomy 8:18*

The purpose of wealth is for God to establish His covenant on the earth. According to this verse, God's covenant cannot be established until you have adequate financial means to accomplish God's instructions for your life. Remember the principles taught in a previous chapter, and understand the difference between an owner and a steward. God is the owner of everything, and therefore, He will equip you with the power to accomplish His instructions. You are a steward. Your responsibility is to oversee what He has entrusted to your care. *He provides the power; you provide the vessel; and through Him will come all wealth.*

Principles for Getting Out of Debt

Here are four principles that I believe will help you get out of debt and become free from being enslaved because of what you owe. Here are the *debt* conquering principles you will learn: 1) Pay as you go. 2) Limit the items you purchase using credit. 3) If you already have credit, don't fall into the "minimum payment trap." 4) Work toward ownership.

I. Pay As You Go, or Don't Go

This was said by an 82-year-old client of mine. He told me about a valuable lesson he learned from his father, dating back to the Depression. He watched his father sitting at the family table, sobbing like a baby because he had no money with which to buy shoes for his children's blistered, worn feet. This was because he had to pay the interest payment due on the family farm. My client said *he has never forgotten what debt had done to his father.* He also remembers the day his father finally paid off the mortgage. He said, "When I handed him the deed to the farm, my father dropped to his knees and wept like a big baby, but this time the tears looked different." My client told me he decided that day that he would never get snared by debt because ownership to him seemed like a better road to travel. If you can't pay cash (exceptions are a house and perhaps a car), you simply can't afford it. The reason being, if you don't have the cash, you will be paying interest on something you couldn't afford in the beginning…thus compounding the problem!

II. Don't Fall Into the Trap of Buying Everything on a Credit Card...

...because you receive an itemized statement at the end of the month. The theory is that this helps keep track of where the money goes. I will tell you where it really goes. *Gone! Gone! Gone!* What happens is that you spend not only on credit, but you spend cash as well. You end up spending more than you would have if you had paid cash to start with. It's easier to charge $100 than to throw down $100 in cold, hard cash. Most people are not disciplined enough to limit themselves to the *"itemized theory."*

III. Do Not Be Preyed Upon by the "Minimum Payment Trap"

Always pay more than the minimum payment. If you pay only the minimum payment, you will end up paying thousands of dollars in interest charges.

IV. Work Toward Ownership

Everything from houses to cars, furniture, vacations, clothes, or any other items you may wish to purchase.

Three Credit Card Debts That I Will Work Towards Paying Off Over the Next 18 Months

1. ____

____

____

____

____

2. ____

____

____

____

____

____

3. ____

____

____

____

Money Will
Not Make
You Happy.

~~~

Not Having
It Can Sure Make
You Miserable.

~ *Todd Coontz* ~

~~~

Myth #7

Money Will Make Me Happy

Money alone will not make you happy! You are probably saying to yourself, "You have just spent six chapters telling me how to get money, and now you conclude with...money will not make me happy? Why not tell me this in the first chapter? I could have saved my money and time!"

Hold on before jumping to conclusions, and think about what I said: "Money *alone* will not make you happy." Happiness is a condition of the heart. If we look at the story of the rich young ruler we can fully understand the real message Jesus taught about the subject of prosperity.

One day an intriguing young man who seemed to have everything came to Jesus to ask Him a sincere question.

> *...Good master, what good thing shall I do, that I may have eternal life?*
>
> *Matthew 19:16*

We must examine this question closely in order to really reveal this man's heart. This man seemed to have everything, but yet he still felt something was missing. I'm sure he may have wondered and even asked himself the question, "What's missing in my life?" He was already doing many good things. In fact, Jesus questioned him about several commandments. "All of these have I kept from my youth up," said the rich young ruler. He must have been searching for perhaps *one more good thing* that he could do which would fill the void he obviously felt.

> *...All these things have I kept from my youth up: what lack I yet?*
>
> *Matthew 19:20*

You may be on a *journey* yourself in search of happiness. Maybe you think that *money* will provide it. You may have tried other avenues to fulfill the void, yet there is still something lacking in your life. Maybe you *think* the pursuit of money and the achievement of wealth will solve the emptiness you are feeling. **Do not be deceived**! *Money will not make you happy!* This young ruler, even though he had achieved wealth, and even though he was keeping most of the commandments religiously, still there was something missing in his life according to his confession, *"What lack I yet?"*

Humanity has always been in search of true happiness. Man's search has led him in many negative directions. Money has been no different. Man's futile efforts to achieve true happiness have almost always concluded with *money* as the solution. In our minds we think, "If I could get a better job, buy a bigger house, drive a nicer car, have more money in the bank," my life would be different, and I would truly be happy. **Money is not the solution for your problem!** *Your problem is spiritual.* Yes, money will afford you more choices. It will give you more leisure along with more opportunities. With money, you can buy more and you can have more. However, it does not mean that *you will be more.* At the end of your search for wealth, when you live in your luxury home, while you drive your expensive automobile, and you take your exotic vacations, you will find that there still remains a void. Something will still be missing. *Spiritual problems cannot be solved by financial solutions!*

All of us have known, met or observed on television programs such as *Lifestyles of the Rich and Famous* wealthy people who seem to have everything, but yet are still searching. I know they are searching because they are continually spending. Money will give you more opportunities to buy more things; however, there will still be a void that only Jesus can fulfill. *Money does not buy happiness*. Think about it for a moment. Do you know someone like this? Maybe it's you. The rich young ruler was not happy. He knew that something was missing, even though he was a good man and had achieved a lifestyle of wealth; there remained a void in his life. *He was still searching.*

Jesus looked into the young man's heart and recognized that *the love of money* was his god. It is important to *note* here that money itself is not wrong. Money only becomes wrong when we value it or place it ahead of God. We can do many good things. Our efforts can be worthy of acknowledgement and even earthly rewards. *However, when Jesus looks at our hearts, what will He see?* What will He find and how many other things have we placed ahead of Him? He said to the young rich ruler:

> *If thou wilt be perfect, go and sell that thou hast, and give to the poor, and thou shalt have treasure in heaven: and come and follow me.*
>
> *Matthew 19:21*

What in the world was Jesus talking about? *Be perfect? Be perfect!* How can this even be possible? Go and sell everything I possess and I will be perfect? *I don't think so!* He was not talking about perfection as we perceive it. The word *"perfect"* used in this verse is more accurately defined as... *to become complete.*

Jesus was giving this young man an opportunity to become complete. *Jesus never had to ask any questions, because He was the Answer.* However, many times He will ask us questions to cause us to search deep in our hearts. It is our responsibility to answer the questions that may be asked of us. No one really knows what is in your heart. Only you can answer certain questions when they are asked.

When God created man, the Bible says ... "*He breathed into man's nostrils the breath of living air.*" Many times humanists will want you to think that man has evolved through evolution, that our ancestry originated from an ape. Really, I think it takes more faith to believe this theory than it does to simply believe God created everything. How about you? What do you believe? What makes man different than any of God's creation is that God breathed into us life. We have been created in the image of God, and we have the life of God abiding in us.

This is why there is a void in our lives when we attempt to satisfy this void without God. Only God can truly satisfy your deepest needs. The emptiness that you may be feeling even now as you read this chapter cannot be filled with **money, fame** or **fortune**...*only God can satisfy!* Not even your good deeds or the wonderful works that you may be doing or have done in the past can satisfy.

When the rich young ruler heard what Jesus said about selling everything he had, *he was startled.* In all of his searching and with all of the distant miles behind him, he had finally arrived at a destination where his Answer was standing there looking at him face to face. He had a choice to make. He was capable of making a decision and no one could make the choice for him. I can imagine that he must have panicked for a moment.

His mind, perhaps, was racing in many directions, trying to grasp at the answer. *All along, the Answer stood right in front of him - Jesus!* Jesus' instruction was **clear.** The young man's *motive* was exposed. His *love* was obvious. He went away sad because he had great wealth.

> *But when the young man heard that saying, he went away sorrowful; for he had great possessions.*
>
> *Matthew 22:19*

This rich young ruler, in all of his searching, simply could not bring himself to the place where he could give up all that he had. He chose his wealth and rejected Jesus.

> *For what is a man profited, if he should gain the whole world, and lose his own soul? or, what shall a man give in exchange for his soul?*
>
> *Matthew 16:26*

Please understand, Jesus did not want his money...He wanted his heart. In fact, I challenge you to find any place in the Bible where God asks anyone to give up their wealth. If they were willing to give it to Him, He would multiply it and return it. God does not want your money and He doesn't need your money. He already owns everything. Whether you acknowledge it or not, your possessions are God's. The only thing that you can truly offer Him... **is your heart.**

Jesus turned to His disciples after the rich young ruler had walked away and said to them:

> *And again I say unto you, it is easier for a camel to go through the eye of a needle, than for a rich man to enter the kingdom of God.*
>
> *Matthew 19:24*

I want to be very clear about what Jesus was saying. As difficult as it may seem, for many years people have believed that Jesus was actually talking about a needle. *Have you ever tried to thread a needle?* I think it would be much more difficult to thread a camel! The eye of a needle that Jesus was talking about was a doorway. It was possible for camels to get through that doorway if they bowed on their knees and crawled through. Jesus was simply saying it is okay to have wealth, it is okay to be rich – just as long as we *bow* our knees to Him first. *Are you willing to bow your knees to Him?*

Money is a tool. Money builds schools, colleges, hospitals and churches. It clothes orphans and feeds the hungry. Money is important. *Money matters.* God does not mind you having money; in fact, He even promises to give you more than just money.

> *And everyone that hath forsaken houses, or brethren, or sisters, or father, or mother, or wife, or children, or lands, for my name's sake, shall receive an* ***hundred fold****, and shall inherit everlasting life.*
>
> *Matthew 19:29*

God's economic system has been designed with checks and balances, rewards and consequences. For every promise that He has ever given, there has always been an action we must take. If we are willing to forsake all and follow Him, He is willing to give everything back to us. *God does not want what is in your hands — He only wants your heart.*

Maybe you have been searching for the answer, and in your diligent search, you are still void and empty. Only Jesus can meet that need. Will you accept Him today? He is willing to accept you. *Money will not make you happy. Jesus will make you* ***complete.***

~ Decision ~

Will You Accept Jesus As Savior of Your Life Today?

The Bible says, "That if thou shalt confess with thy mouth the Lord Jesus, and shalt believe in thine heart that God hath raised Him from the dead, thou shalt be saved. For with the heart man believeth unto righteousness; and with the mouth confession is made unto salvation" (Rom. 10:9-10).

To receive Jesus Christ as Lord and Savior of your life, please pray this prayer from your heart today!

"Dear Jesus, I believe that You died for me and rose again on the third day. I confess I am a sinner. I need Your love and forgiveness. Come into my life, forgive my sins, and give me eternal life. I confess You now as my Lord. Thank You for my salvation, Your peace and joy. Amen."

— —

Yes, Todd, I made a decision to accept Christ as my personal Savior today. Please send me a free copy of your next book.

Name ____

Address ____

City ____

State ____________ Zip _________ Phone _____________

Birthday ____

~ *For Further Information* ~

For additional copies of this book, for further information, or for Todd Coontz's speaking schedule, please write or call:

ROCKWEALTH MINISTRIES
P.O. Box 6177
Aiken, SC 29804-6277

(803) 644-3271

Website:
www.toddcoontz.com